INDIA

A TRUE BOOK

by

Elaine Landau

Children's Press®

A Division of Grolier Publishing

New York London Hong Kong Sydney
Danbury, Connecticut

An Indian elephant

Subject Consultant
Joan Winship
Vice President
The Stanley Foundation

Reading Consultant
Linda Cornwell
Coordinator of School Quality
and Professional Improvement
Indiana State Teachers
Association

Visit Children's Press® on the
Internet at:
http://publishing.grolier.com

Library of Congress Cataloging-in-Publication Data

Landau, Elaine.
    India / Elaine Landau.
        p.   cm. — (A True book)
    Includes index.
    Summary: Surveys the history, geography, people, religions, and economy of India.
    ISBN: 0-516-20982-5 (lib. bdg.)   0-516-26764-7 (pbk.)
    1. India—Juvenile literature.   [1. India]   I. Title.   II. Series.
DS407.L34   1999
954—dc21   98–41179
                                                                               CIP
                                                                                AC

GROLIER
PUBLISHING

Contents

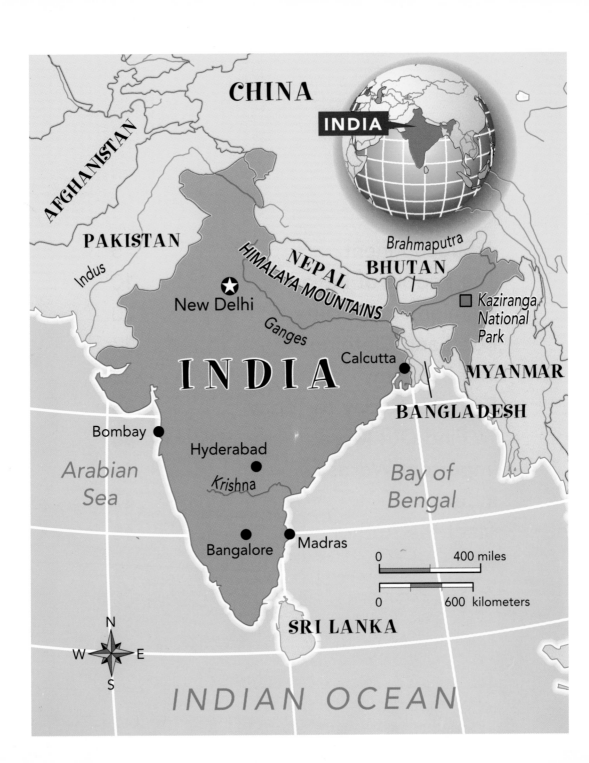

A Subcontinent

India is the world's seventh-largest country. It is located on the continent of Asia. India's population is about one billion people. Various parts of this nation are quite different. Within its borders are snowcapped mountains, tropical forests, fertile farms, and deserts.

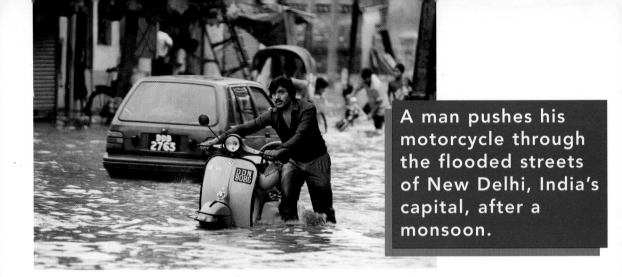

A man pushes his motorcycle through the flooded streets of New Delhi, India's capital, after a monsoon.

India's climate is quite warm. Throughout much of it, temperatures are between 60 and 70 degrees Fahrenheit (15 and 21 degrees Celsius) during the cool season. In the hot season, it's often more than 100 degrees F (38 degrees C). And from July through September, heavy rains called monsoons fall.

India covers about 1,270,000 square miles (3,287,000 square kilometers). Because it's so big and is cut off from the rest of Asia by the Himalaya mountains, it's called a subcontinent. This subcontinent is home to

The Himalaya mountains stretch for 1,500 miles (2,410 km) across Asia through northern India.

The Himalayan brown bear's habitat is in southern Asia.

Himalayan brown bears, tigers, lions, elephants, and a variety of colorful birds. More types of deer are found there than anywhere else on Earth.

In India, you'll also find busy cities crowded with people, buildings, and bazaars. Yet quiet rural areas exist, too.

Kaziranga National Park

Kaziranga National Park is a wildlife preserve where rare and endangered species live in a protected environment. At the park, most of Asia's one-horned rhinoceroses can be found. The park also has tigers, elephants, wild buffalo, crested serpent eagles, and many unusual snakes.

A one-horned rhinoceros

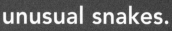
Bengal tigers

The People of India

India's population is a mix of many different people. The two main groups are the Dravidians, who live mostly in the south, and the Indo-Aryans, in northern India. Others in India may be a blend of these two groups. Some are related to India's other early settlers.

Many different groups of people make up India's population.

There are so many varied groups in India that there is also a large number of languages spoken there. Hindi is the official language. But fourteen major languages and hundreds of minor languages are also spoken.

Throughout India, family life is very important. In rural India, young people usually do not date. The husbands or wives of most young Indians are chosen by their parents. In recent years, however, the choice is often made with the young person's agreement.

After marriage, a son and his wife and children often live

This young Hindu couple's wedding ceremony is taking place in New Delhi.

with his parents. Many house-holds in India are made up of grandparents, aunts, uncles, and cousins all living together.

Some Indians are quite wealthy. But many are very poor.

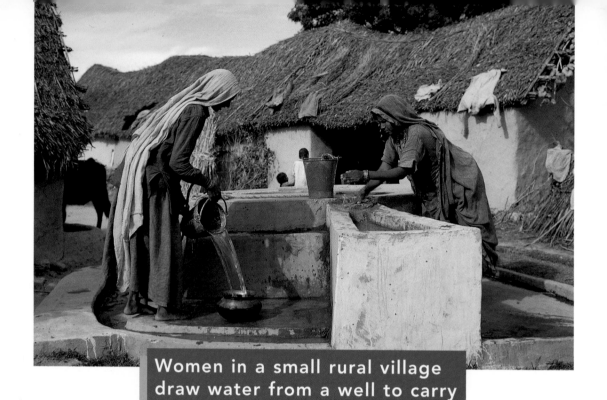

Women in a small rural village draw water from a well to carry back to their homes.

In small villages, families often live in one- or two-room houses with mud floors. There may be no electricity or running water. Women carry water from the village well back to their homes in pots on their heads. A few wealthier villagers live in brick houses. Recently, the Indian government has taken steps to improve life in rural areas. Improvements have been made in health, education, and cleanliness. But there is still much to be done.

There are also large Indian cities where millions of people live. Major cities, such as Calcutta, New Delhi, and Bombay have large stores, air-conditioned restaurants, and tall office buildings. There families live in small brick homes

An aerial view of Bombay, the largest city in India and home to more than eight million people

or apartments with running water and electricity. Other Indian families live in attractive houses with beautiful gardens.

India's cities are filled with stores, carts, bikes, and people. Bazaars with small shops line the streets. Usually the shop owners and their families live behind these shops.

As in other countries, Indian cities also have some large slums. In these slums, homeless people live in the street or in small shelters.

A crowded market street in Bombay

Since overcrowding and cleanliness are problems, disease can spread rapidly. As the population grows, the situation gets worse. The Indian government is trying to find ways to solve these problems.

A family's wealth usually influences the type of education a child receives. Only a small portion of Indian children attend school past sixth grade. Young people often have to work to help their families.

Life is quite different for the children of wealthy Indian families.

Students in some village classrooms (above) do not have desks and chairs. India has more than 4,850 colleges and universities. This (right) is the University of Allahabad.

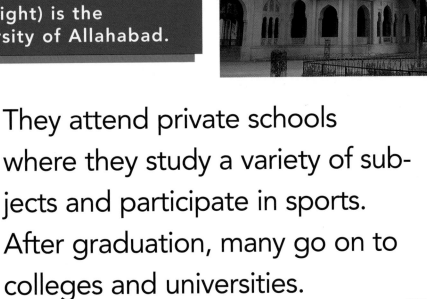

They attend private schools where they study a variety of subjects and participate in sports. After graduation, many go on to colleges and universities.

Religion and Society

Religion is important in India. India is the birthplace of four of the world's religions. They are Hinduism, Buddhism, Jainism, and Sikhism. Most Indians are Hindus. Some are Muslims. Christians and members of other religions can also be found in India.

These Muslims, who make up the second-largest religious group in India, are praying in front of a mosque in Bombay.

Hindu temples can be found throughout India. This one is located in New Delhi.

Hinduism teaches that the soul exists after the body has died. It is reborn in another form. The soul continues to be reborn until it achieves spiritual perfection. Then it enters a higher existence.

Hinduism also teaches care and concern for all living things. Besides not harming humans, Hindus must be careful not to hurt animals. Cows are given special protection.

Hindus consider India's Ganges (GAN-jeez) River sacred. The Ganges is one of the world's longest waterways. Each year,

Hindus bathe in the Ganges River, which they believe is the most sacred river in India.

Hindu pilgrims bathe in its water to purify themselves. The sick and injured go to the Ganges hoping the water will cure them.

Hindus believe that people are born into groups called castes (KASTS). A person's caste can affect who that person marries and is friends with. It will also influence the kind of job a person has.

At the bottom of the caste system are the untouchables. Through the years, this group performed jobs considered unacceptable by Hindus in higher castes. Untouchables were ignored by other Hindus. They couldn't live among members of different castes or even take water from the same wells.

However, the government has outlawed such measures. The 1950 Indian constitution guarantees untouchables full rights as citizens. But some Indians still cling to the old ways and have not helped the untouchables.

Food and Clothing

Popular foods in India may be very different from what you're used to. Most Hindus do not eat beef. Muslims do not eat pork. Vegetable dishes and lamb are most frequently served.

Rice, corn, barley, and *channa* (a type of chickpea)

A collection of Indian foods that includes chapati, chutney, rice, fruit, nuts, and lamb

are basic Indian foods. The most common kind of bread is a round, flat wheat cake known as chapati. Spicy fruit sauces called chutneys are often part of a meal.

Fruits, which are grown throughout the country, are popular. They are used in chutneys and other dishes. Fruits and nuts are ingredients in many of India's desserts.

Traditional Indian clothing also differs from what you might buy in U.S. stores. Some Indian men wear a dhoti (DOH-tee). This is a cloth garment that is draped around a man's waist and legs. It looks like a loose-fitting pair of pants. The shirts worn are also usually long

This man (left) is wearing a dhoti and a long loose shirt, the traditional clothing of Indian men. This Hindu bride (right) is wearing a brightly colored sari made of silk.

and loose. Many Indian men, especially in the countryside, wear turbans on their heads.

Most Indian women wear a length of fabric wrapped around their bodies called a sari (SAH-ree). The saris of wealthy

Indian women may be made of brightly colored silk. Designs of gold and silver thread are usually woven into the fabric. The saris of poor women tend to be made of cotton instead of silk. They are not as fancy.

Not everyone in India wears traditional Indian clothing. Many Indian men—especially those who work in cities—wear clothes that are similar to the ones men in the United States wear. Some women wear dresses instead of saris.

The Economy

Farming is important to India's economy. With such a large population, great amounts of food are needed. Many people in rural India are farmers. Among the crops grown are rice, wheat, and millet.

Farmers also raise cows and buffalo. But because cows are

A farmer plows his field. Farming is an important occupation in India.

sacred to the Hindus, these animals are not eaten. Instead they are used to pull plows and to provide milk.

Over the years, manufacturing in India has increased. India is now one of the largest industrial powers in the world. Iron and steel mills provide materials for

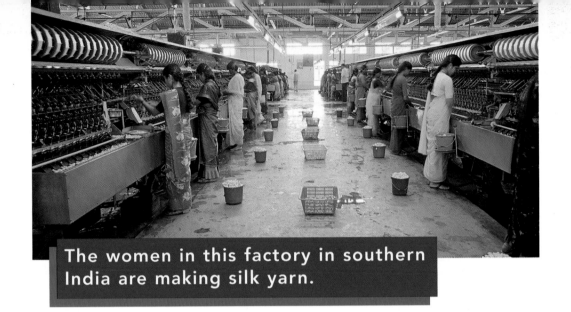

The women in this factory in southern India are making silk yarn.

the cars, bikes, appliances, and machinery made there. Many Indian factories also produce drugs, chemicals, fertilizers, and food products.

Large numbers of Indian textile workers create fine handwoven fabrics. Many work out of their homes making rugs and clothing.

The Taj Mahal

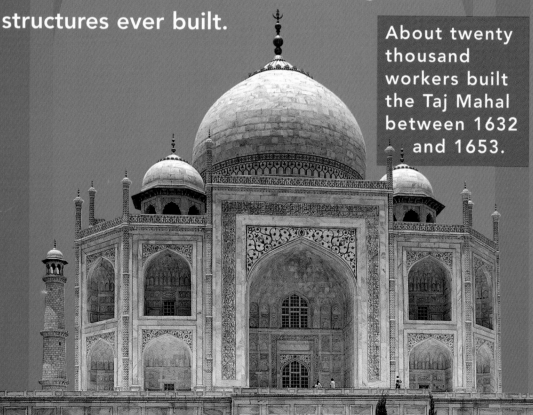

Architecture, the art of designing buildings, is important in India. The country's most famous building is the Taj Mahal. This is a tomb constructed hundreds of years ago by the Indian ruler Shah Jahan for his wife. It has been described as one of the most magnificent structures ever built.

About twenty thousand workers built the Taj Mahal between 1632 and 1653.

From Yesterday to Today

People have been living in India for five thousand years. Throughout its history, it has been invaded by many different groups. In 1858, part of it came under British rule. It was called British India.

As time passed, the Indian people argued that the British

Gandhi (center) leads a group of Indians in a protest in which they sat down and refused to leave until British soldiers carried them away.

denied them important rights and freedoms. As a result, the movement for India's independence began.

The movement's best-known leader was Mohandas Gandhi. Gandhi believed that India's independence could be won

through nonviolent disobedience. This meant that he and
his followers would use only
peaceful ways to disobey the
British. Sometimes they
protested unfair treatment by
sitting down in the street until
they were carried away. They
refused to send their children
to British-controlled schools.
When they were beaten or
even shot at by British soldiers, Gandhi and others still
did not react violently. Their

nonviolent disobedience gained the world's respect.

During India's struggle against the British, problems arose between the Muslims and Hindus. Muslims feared that once India became indepen-dent, the Hindus would treat them unfairly. The Muslims wanted to create their own nation in a separate part of India. They wanted to call their new country Pakistan, which means "Land of the Pure."

In this 1947 photograph, Indians in the city of Calcutta celebrate the country's independence.

In 1946, Britain agreed to free India. But the Muslims insisted on having their own country. Indian and British leaders eventually agreed to give part of India to the Muslims. In August 1947, India and Pakistan became separate independent countries.

Today, India is a democratic nation whose leaders are elected by the people. There is a Parliament, which makes the country's laws. The prime minister is the leader of the government. There is also an Indian president, but the president doesn't have a lot of power.

Members of India's Parliament, who meet in a building called Parliament House, in New Delhi

Through the years, India has had difficulty getting along with its neighbor countries, China and Pakistan. So India spent a lot of money to find ways to defend itself from attacks. In May 1974, India tested its first nuclear bomb. But Indian leaders claimed that the country would not build many nuclear weapons.

In May 1998, India exploded five nuclear bombs underground. This action angered the leaders of nations throughout the world. They feared it might encourage

One of many groups who gathered in May 1998 to support India's underground nuclear tests.

the building of even more nuclear weapons. However, the Indian prime minister has said that India may sign a treaty that keeps countries from testing nuclear weapons.

India is the world's largest democracy. It has a proud tradition of nonviolence. Hopefully, this tradition will continue into the future.

To Find Out More

Here are some additional resources to help you learn more about the nation of India:

 **Books**

Bailey, Donna. **India.** Raintree Steck-Vaughn, 1990.

Ganeri, Anita. **Hindu.** Children's Press, 1996.

Ganeri, Anita. **The Indian Subcontinent.** Franklin Watts, 1994.

Haskins, Jim. **Count Your Way Through India.** Carolrhoda Books, 1992.

Hermes, Jules M. **The Children of India.** Carolrhoda Books, 1993.

Kaur, Sharon. **Food In India.** Rourke, 1999.

Lewin, Ted. **Sacred River.** Clarion, 1995.

Prior, Katherine. **Indian Subcontinent.** Franklin Watts, 1997.

Organizations and Online Sites

India-U.S. Foundation

12450 Fair Lakes Circle
Suite 370
Fairfax, VA 22033

Encourages and promotes interaction and understanding between the people of India and the United States. Conducts programs and services for children.

Indian Heritage

http://www.saigon.com/ heritage

Here you'll find information about Indian music and dance, gods and goddesses, painting and sculpture, and temples and architecture. There are also links to other sites.

Pitara for Kids

http://www.pitara.com

Pitara is a Hindi word that means something similar to "a chest full of surprises." This site, designed especially for children, contains books, stories, folk tales, and activities with an Indian perspective.

We Are India

http://weareindia.com

Created to popularize Indian culture, traditions, and art forms, this site contains photos and links to other sites.

Important Words

bazaar a marketplace or group of shops

continent one of the seven large land masses of the earth

democracy a way of governing a country in which the people choose their leaders in elections

inhabitant someone who lives in a particular area

irrigate to supply water to crops by artificial means, such as channels and pipes

rural having to do with the countryside or a farming area

species a particular type of plant or animal

treaty a formal agreement between two or more countries

turban a head covering made by winding a long scarf around the head

Index

Meet the Author

Elaine Landau has a Bachelor of Arts degree in English and Journalism from New York University and a Masters degree in Library and Information Science from Pratt Institute. She has worked as a newspaper reporter, children's book editor, and a youth services librarian, but especially enjoys writing for young people.

Ms. Landau has written more than one hundred nonfiction books on various topics. She lives in Miami, Florida, with her husband Norman and son, Michael.

DUNCAN

DATE DUE

DUNCAN